Cajun Rules

by

G.A. (Gaboon) Trahan

Courtesy of Norman Kemmer and his life with the
American Pit Bull Terrier

Mitch Kemmer

Cajun Rules
by Mitch Kemmer

© 2018 Mitch Kemmer

ISBN: 978-1-7328283-2-2

Printed in the United States

All rights reserved. No part of this book may be reproduced in any form or by any means without permission in writing from Mitch Kemmer, except for the inclusion of brief quotations in a review.

Cajun Rules

by

G.A. (Gaboon) Trahan

PRICE $1.00

Galbert "Gaboon" A. Trahan
1894 - 1975
Lifelong Law Enforcement Officer;
Chief of Police, 1936-1939.

Norman Kemmer purchased this copy of Gaboon Trahan's Cajun Rules in the late 1960s as he first entered the sport of Dog Fighting. We were told by Floyd B. that Trahan wrote this set of rules in 1954. All of my life men have said, "We are going by the Cajun Rules", but truly few of them knew what they said. My father carried his set in his shirt pocket to every match. His original set is the only original copy that I personally have ever seen straight from the 'Trahan Printing Press'. I have been asked by many who are fans of the History of the American Pit Bull Terrier, to copy this Historical Artifact to the best of my ability and make it available to the public. This copy is meant for those interested in the History of the Sport, and not in any way meant to be used in any illegal activities. I am publishing this as a tribute to Gaboon Trahan as the author of these rules, and to Norman Kemmer as the best Referee I ever saw in the game. So to the author of these rules, and best enforcer of these rules, I salute you.

RULE 1. Size of pit, optional: to be square with sides 2 feet high, scratch line 12 feet apart.

RULE 2. Referee to be chosen before the dogs are weighed in or washed and referee to conduct the contest according to these rules and his decision to be final.

RULE 3. Referee to see the dogs weighed at time agreed on and if either dog is over top weight agreed on he loses the forfeit money.

RULE 4. Parties to toss coin to see who shall wash first, each party to furnish two clean towels and a blanket.

RULE 5. If requested to do so the referee shall search the person named to wash the dogs and then have him bare his arm to the elbow and wash both dogs in the same warm water and rinse them each in his half of the warm clean water provided for that purpose.

RULE 6. As the dogs are washed clean and dried they shall be turned over to their handlers and at once taken to their corners of the pit as designated by the referee and the referee must search handlers for means of foul play and see that he bares his arms to the elbow before he receives his dog and must keep his arms bare in such a manner during the contest.

RULE 7. The dog's owner or his representative shall be allowed at all times to be near his dog and watch to see that no harm is done him, and each owner shall be allowed to name a man or himself watch his opponent's dog and handler at all times to see he is given no unfair advantage.

RULE 8. Either dog's owner, handler or watcher if he sees anything wrong must at once appeal to the referee and get his decision. And if any handler, watcher or owner violates any of these rules and thereby favors either dog the dog so favored must at once be declared the loser.

RULE 9. The interested parties shall choose a timekeeper at the pit side.

RULE 10. The dogs are placed in their corners of the pit, opposite corners, faces turned from each other and only the dogs and their handlers inside the pit. Then the referee shall say, "Face your dogs". Each handler must always show his dog full head and shoulders between his legs. The referee says, "Let go", but the handlers must never push or shove their dogs and handlers shall not leave their corners until the dogs are together.

Rule 11. Now when one of the dogs turns his head and shoulders away from his opponent after the fight is on it is a turn, whether they are in holds or free, and the handler must claim the turn and the referee must allow the claim if he believes it is a turn or the referee must call the first fair turn he sees whether the handler claims it or not and when the referee calls a turn he shall say. "Handle your dogs", and each handler must pick up his dog as soon as he can without breaking a hold. Handlers carry their dog to their respective corners immediately on picking them up, keeping the dog's face turned away from the center of the pit. Twenty-five seconds after the dogs are carried to their corners the referee shall say, "Face your dogs". Then the handlers must show their dog's head and shoulders between their legs, facing the center of the pit. The dog that turned first must scratch first. In five seconds more the referee shall say: "Let go", then the dog that made the first turn must be turned loose by his handler and this dog must go across and mouth the other dog. If, when he is turned loose he refuses to start at once or if he stops on the way over, or if he fails to reach his opponent, he has lost the fight and the referee must declare his opponent the winner.

A handler is allowed to release his dog at any time he sees fit after the dog whose turn it is to cross has started over. He must turn him loose when the dogs touch each other. He is not compelled to until then.

RULE 12. (a) If neither dog has made a turn and they cease to fight after 60 seconds of no action the down dog is to scratch first, if he makes his scratch the fight is on and they shall scratch in turns until the contest is decided.

(b) If the down dog fails to scratch the other dog is to scratch to win. If he fails to scratch the contest shall be declared a draw by the referee.

(c) No handler is to handle his dog until ordered by referee, if he does, it shall be called a foul and he is to forfeit the contest to his opponent.

(d) No flash pictures or hitting on the pit side shall be allowed unless agreed upon by the two contestants.

RULE 13. After the dogs are together this time either handler is allowed to pick up his dog when they are not in holds, if ordered by referee. If he tries for a pick up and either dog has a hold he must turn him loose at once. If he catches his dog up free both handlers must handle their dogs at once.

Take their dogs to their corners and proceed same as at the first turn, except this time the dog which went across before is allowed to remain in his corner while his opponent makes a scratch, or goes across, and they alternate or take it turn about in this manner until one of them is declared the winner under these rules. The referee pays no attention to the turns after the first scratch.

RULE 14. If one of the dogs fangs himself, that is, if he gets his teeth hung in his own lip, his handler is allowed to unfang him. If the dogs have to be separated for this they are turned loose again both at the same time within two feet of each other in the center of the pit.

RULE 15. No sponging shall be allowed, and no towels or anything else taken into the pit by the handlers except a bottle of drink for his dog and a fan to cool him with. The handlers must taste their dogs drink before the referee to show that it contains no poison.

RULE 16. If the handler of either dog is seen to take anything from anyone on the outside of the pit he is to lose the battle. Each part shall have the right to put a man near his opponent's corner to watch the handler. Should he see the handler put anything on his dog he may appeal to the referee and if the referee finds anything on the dog he is to lose the battle.

RULE 17. Should either handler leave the pit with his dog before the referee renders his decision he is to lose the battle.

RULE 18. The handlers shall be allowed to encourage their dogs by voice or hand-clapping or snapping of fingers, but must not touch their dogs or use foul, dirty methods, by saving their dogs from hard fall or keeping the other handler away from his dog, or in any other way act unfairly. The Referee must decide the battle against the one who does so.

RULE 19. Should the police interfere the referee to name the next meeting place.

GABOON TRAHAN

Summary

Always remember when it comes to the rules of the Sport, that any rules can be altered if agreed on by both parties and made clear to the Referee prior to the beginning of the match. 'Out of Hold Counts' are a common thing agreed on that the rules do not stress. Also a 'Count' on the scratch is a common number agreed on prior to the beginning of combat. But know that any rules agreed upon by both parties can over ride the official rules. The rules are basically common sense and meant to allow either dog the opportunity to stop the combat at any point that he, the dog, has had enough. Remember it is a Sport, and as long as all parties involved conduct themselves like Gentleman it will remain so.

Thanks again to Gaboon Trahan and Norman Kemmer for this Historical Document used to make this information available to Dog Men world wide.

Norman Kemmer and Kemmer's Macho

Mitch Kemmer and Kemmer's Devan

www.ingramcontent.com/pod-product-compliance
Lightning Source LLC
Chambersburg PA
CBHW041400160426
42811CB00101B/1490